REV SR. IMMACULATA

Novena to st Charbel Makhlouf

The Biography, Spiritual legacy and prayers to Saint Charbel Makhlouf

Dedication:

This book is dedicated to the memory of Saint Charbel Makhlouf, whose life and spirituality continue to inspire and touch the hearts of people around the world. It is also dedicated to all those who have found solace, guidance, and miracles through their devotion to Saint Charbel.

Contents

I

Part One

Novena to St. Charbel Makhlouf

Chapter 1

Introduction to the Novena

Recognizing the Influence of Novenas

Novenas have a special position in the world of spirituality and devotion. For generations, believers have treasured these nine-day prayer cycles as a powerful means of connecting with God and asking for intercession on their behalf. Saint Charbel Makhlouf, a venerated saint whose life and miracles continue to inspire and transform lives, is the subject of one such potent novena.

A novena is a set of prayers that are said over the course of nine days. In religious traditions, the number nine has special meaning because it is associated with wholeness and fullness. It is comparable to the nine months of pregnancy, the nine angelic choirs, and the nine days of prayer the Apostles engaged in between Christ's ascension and the Holy Spirit's arrival at Pentecost. This numerical pattern highlights the novena practice's intentionality and spiritual significance.

Numerous people seeking spiritual comfort, healing, direction, and intercession retain a particular place in their hearts for the novena to Saint Charbel Makhlouf. A modest Lebanese monk named Saint Charbel, also referred to as Mar Charbel, lived in the 19th century. His life was marked by intense devotion, strict asceticism, and a close relationship with God.

Saint Charbel, who was born Youssef Antoun Makhlouf in the Lebanese town of Beqaa-Kafra, was called to the monastic life as a result. He became a member of the Lebanese Maronite Order and adopted a life of seclusion, prayer, and sacrifice. He gained notoriety for his virtues, healing miracles, and profound spiritual insight because of his unwavering dedication to the path of holiness.

The Saint Charbel Makhlouf Novena is a concentrated and deliberate manner to invoke his intercession and feel the trans-forming influence of his spirituality. By participating in this nine-day prayer retreat, people allow God's love and blessings to flow through the saint's relationship with Him.

Participants in the novena are encouraged to focus on particular prayers, consider the life and miracles of Saint Charbel, and com-mit their wishes to his intercession during this time. Through these prayers, people forge a strong spiritual connection with Saint Charbel, becoming more familiar with his teachings, virtues, and the intense love he had for both God and others.

Novenas' strength comes from more than just praying them over and over; it also comes from the pray-er's faith, commitment, and sincerity. This devoted commitment is what causes hearts to open, miracles to be seen, and life-changing events to take place. People can express their deepest longings, pour out their souls, and find a hallowed space to do so during a novena to Saint Charbel Makhlouf.

May your heart be receptive to the grace and benefits that await you as you begin this novena to Saint Charbel Makhlouf. May you honor the spiritual legacy of this revered saint during the next nine days, benefit from his intercession for you in your need for healing, direction, and spiritual growth.

For each day of the novena, we will provide instructions and reflections in the chapters that follow as we delve deeper into the life and miracles of Saint Charbel Makhlouf. Let's take this sacred trip together and learn about the deep spiritual connection that awaits us in our devotion to Saint Charbel Makhlouf.

- Why Do We Pray to Saint Charbel Makhlouf?

As a way to communicate with the divine and ask for comfort, direction, and intercession, prayer is a universal language of the soul. Saint Charbel Makhlouf has become a venerated figure in Catholicism and the Maronite tradition, enticing the devout to seek his potent intercession. But why do so many individuals pray to Saint Charbel?

1. An Ascetic and Holistic Life:
The life of Saint Charbel Makhlouf was marked by persistent

devotion, extreme sanctity, and strict austerity. He isolated himself from the world's distractions as a hermit monk in the Lebanese mountains so that he may devote himself entirely to God. His dedication to a life of prayer, fasting, and self-denial demonstrated his sincere desire to get closer to God and to exhibit Christ's values. People pray to Saint Charbel in order to obtain his intercession because they are inspired by his holy life and the qualities he displayed.

2. Extraordinary Cure and Intercession:

The miracles and healings attributed to Saint Charbel Makhlouf have continued long after his passing. Numerous people have benefited by his intercession physically, emotionally, and spiritually both during his time on Earth and in the present. His reputation as a potent intercessor has been solidified by these remarkable interventions, which have led others to turn to him for assistance when they are in need. Saint Charbel's ongoing presence and active involvement in the lives of Christians are attested to by the testimonies of many who have received healing through his intercession.

3. Spiritual insight and direction:

The spirituality of Saint Charbel Makhlouf was based on abiding prayer and close communion with God. His life was characterized by significant mystical encounters and mystical moments with the divine. He provided insights into the spiritual life through his teachings and lifestyle, assisting others in finding their own paths to purity and oneness with God. Many people seek the wisdom and spiritual direction of Saint Charbel in order to navigate the difficulties and conundrums of life.

3. Popular piety and devotion:

As devotion to Saint Charbel Makhlouf has developed through time, it has reached Christians all over the world and has beyond the borders of Lebanon. Devotion to Saint Charbel has become an essential component of their religious practice as more people have come to understand the strength of his intercession and seen the results of his spirituality. Believers derive strength from the social devotion and shared faith, joining the many faithful who have received comfort and grace through prayer to Saint Charbel.

5. The Illustration of Modesty and Holiness:

The life of the saint Charbel Makhlouf serves as an example for believers desiring to advance in holiness. Those desiring to strengthen their personal relationship with God find great comfort in his humility, simplicity, and detachment from materialistic goals. People who pray to Saint Charbel hope to adopt his virtues and change their lives in accordance with the example he provided.

An act of faith, trust, and hope is praying to Saint Charbel Makhlouf. It is a recognition of his sanctity, his constant presence, and his prayer on behalf of those who turn to him for assistance. By asking this cherished saint to pray for them, Christians invite him to do so by opening their hearts to the grace and blessings that flow through them.

Let us approach our prayers as we begin this novena to Saint Charbel Makhlouf with sincerity, trust, and the conviction that his intercession can bring relief, direction, and transformation to our lives. May our devotion to Saint Charbel strengthen our relationship with God and bring us nearer to His abounding grace.

- The Promise and Purpose of the Novena

The nine-day novena to Saint Charbel Makhlouf is more than just a collection of prayers; it also holds a significant promise and goal. It is crucial for Christians to understand the importance of the novena and the benefits that await those who do it with faith and dedication as they set out on this spiritual journey.

1. Requesting Divine Intervention and Favor:

The Saint Charbel Makhlouf Novena is a potent way to ask for his intercession and invoke his help in our lives. We appreciate his closeness to God and his capacity to act as our advocate by entrusting him with our intentions, needs, and wishes. We give ourselves up to the heavenly aid and favor that Saint Charbel may provide for us via the novena.

2. Strengthening Our Bond with God:

A methodical and concentrated approach to strengthen our connection with God is through praying the novena. We are encouraged to become closer to the holy presence as we contemplate the prayers and think on the character traits and life of Saint Charbel. Through the novena, we may develop a closer relationship with God, align our hearts with His will, and increase our faith, trust, and love.

3. Growing spiritually and through change:

The novena offers a chance for spiritual and personal development in addition to soliciting assistance from others. By participating in the nine days of prayer, we enable the Holy Spirit to operate inside us and shape us in accordance with God's divine design. As we continue the novena, we could feel renewed on the inside, have more faith, have our wounds healed, and have our spiritual life grow.

4. Discovering Saint Charbel's Spiritual Legacy

We immerse ourselves in Saint Charbel Makhlouf's spiritual tradition by participating in the novena. We examine his character, qualities, lessons, and miracles, letting his example motivate and direct us. We get to know Saint Charbel personally via the novena, developing a spiritual bond with him and adopting the principles and virtues he exemplified.

5. Growing Faith and Hope in God's Providence:

The Saint Charbel Novena instills in us a spirit of optimism and faith in God's providence. As we entrust Saint Charbel with our wants and intentions, we release our cares and concerns to God, trusting that He hears our prayers and acts in accordance with His heavenly wisdom. The novena takes on a new meaning as a transformational experience of faith, confidence, and trust in God's tender care.

The spiritual fruits that the novena may produce in our lives are where its promise rests. In the course of the nine days of prayer, we may see answered prayers, meet healing, receive wisdom in making challenging choices, and profoundly feel God's adoring presence. Beyond the immediate benefits, the novena serves as a road to spiritual development, strengthening of faith, and connection with God.

Let us keep onto the hope and goal this novena to Saint Charbel Makhlouf brings as we begin. May us live each day with faith, persistence, and an open heart, hoping that the grace of God and the intercession of Saint Charbel will draw us nearer to Him and bring graces into our lives.

Chapter 2

The Life and Miracles of Saint Charbel Makhlouf

- Early Life and Background

To really comprehend and appreciate Saint Charbel Makhlouf's life and miracles, it is necessary to go into his early years and the formative circumstances that moulded him into the beloved saint he would become.

Saint Charbel was born on May 8, 1828, in the little town of Beqaa-Kafra in Northern Lebanon as Youssef Antoun Makhlouf. He was born into a devout Maronite Catholic family, which instilled in him a great love for God as well as a solid foundation in the Christian religion from a young age.

Youssef's upbringing was characterised by simplicity, devotion, and an innate need to pray. He exhibited spiritual depth and introspection, often spending long hours alone, communing with God in the grandeur of nature that surrounded his town. These early encounters paved the way for his deep spirituality and close contact with the divine.

Youssef's father enrolled him in the local Catholic school to get a formal education, recognizing his son's great spiritual vocation. Despite his intellectual talents, Youssef felt a stronger draw toward a life of prayer and devotion, longing to devote himself completely to God. His longing for sanctity drove him to make a life-changing decision: to abandon his family and go on a monastic adventure.

Youssef joined the Monastery of Our Lady of Mayfouq at the age of 23, where he dedicated himself to the monastic life. He assumed the monastic habit and the name Charbel, after a second-century martyr. Charbel adopted a life of extreme austerity, prayer, and self-denial from the time he wore the habit.

Within the monastery, Charbel maintained an extraordinary zeal for prayer and spiritual progress. He immersed himself in the rich liturgical legacy of the Church, delving thoroughly into the ancient rituals of the Maronite tradition. His days were spent with meditation, hard work, and commitment to the monastic discipline.

As his monastic journey proceeded, Charbel developed a strong desire for a more solitary and hermitic lifestyle. This desire prompted him to apply for permission to live as a hermit on the monastery grounds. Recognizing the sincerity of his desire, the monastery officials approved his request, and Charbel retired to a neighboring little hermitage.

Charbel developed his life of prayer, fasting, and self-mortification amid the seclusion of his hermitage. He chose a life of quiet and seclusion, committing himself fully to God's communion. Years in isolation honed his spiritual skills, establishing his relationship with the divine and prepared him for the momentous task that lay ahead of him.

Charbel's sanctity and spiritual knowledge drew notice even in his solitude. Pilgrims and monks alike sought him advice on topics of religion, spirituality, and practical life concerns. Charbel's gentle attitude, deep spirituality, and ability to provide compassionate counsel made an indelible effect on those who met him.

Saint Charbel Makhlouf's early life and background lay the groundwork for his destiny as a recognized saint. His upbringing in a devout family, his great passion for prayer and solitude, and his unshakeable devotion to a life of holiness formed his character and prepared him for the miraculous and spiritual influence he would have on many souls later in life.

We shall look at Charbel's spiritual journey inside the monastery, his teachings and virtues, and the remarkable miracles that happened both during and after his death in the following chapters. Join us as we explore further into this revered saint's life and legacy, uncovering the significant influence he continues to have on the spiritual lives of Christians all around the globe.

- Call to Monastic Life

The vocation to monastic life is a heavenly summons that draws selected people into a life of great spiritual devotion and contemplation. This summons was apparent for Saint Charbel Makhlouf, and it impacted the course of his life, leading him to become one of the most venerated saints in the Maronite religion.

From an early age, Charbel had a strong desire for prayer, solitude, and closer connection with God. This inner calling got stronger and more forceful as he grew older. Charbel's heart burned with a longing to abandon the world's diversions and devote himself entirely to a life of holiness and intimate contact with the divine.

The vocation to monastic life is often preceded by a time of discernment in which persons seek spiritual mentorship and engage in contemplative meditation. This procedure included Charbel seeking advice from his family, parish priest, and others who noticed his strong spiritual devotion.

Charbel took the bold choice to answer the call he had felt since boyhood, with the support and blessing of his loved ones. He joined the Monastery of Our Lady of Mayfouq in Lebanon's highlands when he was 23 years old. Charbel would begin his lifetime path of self-surrender and profound connection with God inside the walls of this monastery.

Charbel accepted the monastic way of life wholeheartedly upon joining the monastery. He readily accepted the monastic rule's rigors, which comprised a strict schedule of communal prayer, liturgical services, physical work, and personal ascetic disciplines. Charbel tried to free himself of worldly attachments and build a rich internal existence via these techniques.

Charbel's dedication to the monastic life was immediately clear. He was recognized for his uncompromising obedience to his superiors, humility in doing menial jobs, and unshakable dedication to the monastery's community prayer life. His sincere love for God and his fellow monks shone through in all he did, winning him the respect and adoration of everyone around him.

Charbel's desire for a more isolated and quiet existence became greater with time. This yearning prompted him to apply for permission to live as a hermit on the monastery grounds. His superiors offered him the isolation he sought, recognizing the depth of his vocation and his unshakeable dedication to monastic values.

Charbel increased his practice of prayer, fasting, and self-mortification in his hermitage. He saw seclusion as a chance for uninterrupted communication with God, and devoted himself to never-ending prayer and contemplation. Charbel's spiritual skills grew and his oneness with the divine increased in this secluded environment.

Charbel's spiritual influence was felt outside the hermitage, despite his choice of solitude. Pilgrims and other monks sought him out because of his holiness and ability to provide spiritual instruction and solace. Charbel's gentle attitude and deep insights impacted the hearts of everybody who met him, leaving a lasting impression of his holiness.

Saint Charbel Makhlouf's personality and mission were formed by the vocation to monastic life. It enabled him to devote himself entirely to a life of prayer, contemplation, and self-surrender. Charbel's example continues to encourage others to respond to the call to greater spiritual commitment and to embark on the transformational path of monasticism.

- Charbel's Spiritual Journey

The life of Saint Charbel Makhlouf was defined by a profound spiritual journey—a road of intimate connection with God, transformational experiences, and constant devotion. Charbel went on a unique journey for spiritual unification and personal connection with the divine via his dedication to prayer, austerity, and the pursuit of holiness.

1. Adopting a Contemplative Lifestyle:
   Charbel embraced the contemplative life from the beginning of his monastic journey. He realized that genuine unity with God called for calm, stillness, and an open heart. Charbel attempted to rid himself of worldly distractions via hours of prayer and meditation, shifting his concentration inward to converse with the Divine Presence.

2. The Effectiveness of Liturgical Prayer:
   Liturgical prayer is very important in the Maronite tradition.

Charbel engaged himself in his faith's rich liturgical tradition, completely engaging in the monastic community's prayers, chants, and rites. The liturgy provided a conduit for Charbel to connect his heart with the entire Church, expressing his praise and prayer in unison with Christians across time and place.

3. Self-Denial and Fasting:

In the spiritual life, Charbel recognized the transformational potential of fasting and self-denial. He wanted to cleanse his passions and remove himself from worldly attachments by freely accepting bodily hardship and mortification. Charbel attempted to align his will with God's via self-discipline, fostering a spirit of obedience and submission.

4. Union with God on the inside:

Charbel's spiritual path was centered on his heartfelt desire for oneness with God. He want to know God not only about God, but to know God personally. He wanted to enter the presence of the Divine via contemplative prayer, enabling God's love to alter him from inside. Charbel's relationship with God pervaded every part of his life, becoming the driving force behind his actions and decisions.

5. The Virtues in Action:

The development of virtues was fundamental to Charbel's spiritual path. He aspired to live a life of humility, simplicity, and obedience, traits he saw shown in Christ's life. Charbel felt that real holiness needed character modification, a progressive conformity to the image of Christ. He cultivated characteristics that were trademarks of his holiness by daily practice and dependence on God's mercy.

6. Divine Favors and Mystical Encounters:

Charbel's spiritual path was peppered with mystical experiences and heavenly graces. He had deep experiences of spiritual ecstasy in which he was carried above the constraints of the physical world and immersed in God's presence. These meetings confirmed his chosen path, increasing his faith and encouraging others who observed the brightness of his spiritual experiences.

Charbel's spiritual path demonstrated his unshakeable dedication to the pursuit of God and his readiness to entirely submit to the divine will. Through his experience, he became a vehicle for God's grace and an encouragement to other Christians.

- Notable Miracles and Interventions

Saint Charbel Makhlouf was linked with several miracles and heavenly interventions during his life and even after his death. These unusual happenings attest to his holiness and the strong intercession he continues to provide to all who come to him in faith and request.

1. Healing Wonders:

Saint Charbel's capacity to intercede for bodily healing is one of the most notable parts of his miraculous fame. Countless people have experienced miraculous healings from sicknesses and maladies after requesting his intercession. The accounts of healing ascribed to Saint Charbel range from potentially incurable ailments to crippling afflictions.

2. Sight Restoration:

The restoration of sight to the blind is one of the miracles credited to Saint Charbel. Many people with different visual problems have experienced a rapid and inexplicable restoration of their eyesight after praying to Saint Charbel. These narratives continue to inspire faith and bear witness to his amazing involvement.

3. Spiritual Transformations and Conversions:

Saint Charbel's power goes beyond physical healing. Many people have claimed remarkable conversions and spiritual changes as a result of his intercession. People who were lost, hurting, or disconnected from their religion discovered fresh hope, faith, and purpose after seeking the guidance of Saint Charbel. His intercession has brought people closer to God and enhanced their devotion to a holy life.

4. Intercession in Extreme Circumstances:

Saint Charbel is also recognized for his intercession in times of need. Numerous people who have faced apparently insurmountable obstacles, crises, or grave situations have resorted to Saint Charbel in their hour of need and have experienced unexpected aid, direction, and deliverance. His intervention has offered many oppressed by overwhelming situations relief, calm, and resolution.

5. Posthumous Wonders:

Saint Charbel's intercession continues to yield fruit even after his death. Over the years, reports of postmortem miracles due to his intercession have been chronicled. Healings, conversions, and other unusual manifestations attest to Saint Charbel's continuous spiritual presence and intercessory ability.

Saint Charbel Makhlouf's noteworthy miracles and interventions attest to his holiness and one-of-a-kind relationship with the almighty. Numerous people have been transformed by God's love and compassion as a result of his prayer.

Chapter 3

Praying with Saint Charbel Makhlouf: A Guide to the Novena

- Preparation for the Novena

B efore commencing on the strong Novena to Saint Charbel Makhlouf, it is important to spiritually and psychologically prepare oneself. The preparatory phase lays the groundwork for a productive and transforming encounter, enabling us to deepen our relationship with the saint and open our hearts to his intercession.

1. Recognizing the Novena:

Begin by learning what a novena is and why it is important in the Catholic faith. A novena is a nine-day time of concentrated prayer and devotion, usually aimed towards a certain saint or component of the religion. It is a chance to seek the saint's intercession and to develop in faith through persistent prayer.

2. Research Saint Charbel Makhlouf:

Take the time to explore and understand about Saint Charbel

Makhlouf's life, virtues, and miracles. Learn about his life, teachings, and the influence he has had on the lives of Christians. This knowledge will strengthen your bond with him and increase your commitment throughout the novena.

3. Establish a Goal:

As you begin the novena, consider your particular aims and aspirations. In what areas of your life are you looking for direction, healing, or transformation? Offer these requests to Saint Charbel, relying on his intercession and God's grace to work in your life.

4. Collect Resources:

Obtain a copy of the novena prayers as well as any other materials that may help you in your devotion to Saint Charbel for the nine days. A prayer book, a picture or image of Saint Charbel, or any other aids that connect with your spiritual practice may be included.

5. Establish a Sacred Space:

Make a holy location where you may pray and do the novena without interruptions. Set up a small altar or table with the picture of Saint Charbel, candles, and any other symbols or artifacts that inspire devotion and help you concentrate on the saint's presence.

6. Develop a Faithful Attitude:

Prepare for the novena with an open and eager heart, fostering confidence and trust in God's providence. Consider Saint Charbel to be there and willing to intervene on your behalf. Allow yourself to be open to the graces that will come as a result of the novena.

7. Develop a Perseverance Spirit:
Recognize that a novena is a commitment that lasts nine days. Accept a persevering attitude, knowing that regular prayer and commitment will strengthen your relationship with Saint Charbel and enable you to have a more meaningful experience of his intercession.

By spiritually and intellectually preparing yourself, you provide a fertile ground for the novena to take root and bring fruit in your life. Accept this preparation period as a chance to prepare for the transforming encounter with Saint Charbel Makhlouf in the next days of prayer and devotion.

- Day 1: Prayer :

In the name of the Father, and of the Son, and of the Holy Spirit.

R. Amen.

God, who is infinitely holy and is exalted in your saints, who gave the hermit monk St. Charbel the courage to withdraw from the world in order to live fully in his hermitage the monastic virtues of poverty, obedience, and chastity, we implore you to give us the grace to love and serve you as he did.

(Say your intentions here...)

Lord Almighty, who has shown the power of St. Charbel's intercession by many miracles and graces, grant our volunteers the grace to live a glorious mission and return home strong in faith and filled with fervent charity. We beseech you through his prayer

R. Amen

St. Charbel, intercede for us.

Say 1: Our Father... Say 1: Hail Mary... Say 1: Glory Be...

* * *

- Day 2: Prayer :

In the name of the Father, and of the Son, and of the Holy Spirit.

R. Amen.

God, who is infinitely holy and is exalted in your saints, who gave the hermit monk St. Charbel the courage to withdraw from the world in order to live fully in his hermitage the monastic virtues of poverty, obedience, and chastity, we implore you to give us the grace to love and serve you as he did.

(Say your intentions here...)

Lord Almighty, who has shown the power of St. Charbel's intercession by many miracles and graces, grant our volunteers the grace to live a glorious mission and return home strong in faith and filled with fervent charity. We beseech you through his prayer

R. Amen

St. Charbel, intercede for us.

Say 1: Our Father... Say 1: Hail Mary... Say 1: Glory Be...

* * *

- Day 3: Prayer :

In the name of the Father, and of the Son, and of the Holy Spirit.

R. Amen.

God, who is infinitely holy and is exalted in your saints, who gave the hermit monk St. Charbel the courage to withdraw from the world in order to live fully in his hermitage the monastic virtues of poverty, obedience, and chastity, we implore you to give us the grace to love and serve you as he did.

(Say your intentions here...)

Lord Almighty, who has shown the power of St. Charbel's intercession by many miracles and graces, grant our volunteers the grace to live a glorious mission and return home strong in faith and filled with fervent charity. We beseech you through his prayer

R. Amen

St. Charbel, intercede for us.

Say 1: Our Father... Say 1: Hail Mary... Say 1: Glory Be...

* * *

- Day 4: Prayer :

In the name of the Father, and of the Son, and of the Holy Spirit.

R. Amen.

God, who is infinitely holy and is exalted in your saints, who gave the hermit monk St. Charbel the courage to withdraw from the world in order to live fully in his hermitage the monastic virtues of poverty, obedience, and chastity, we implore you to give us the grace to love and serve you as he did.

(Say your intentions here...)

Lord Almighty, who has shown the power of St. Charbel's intercession by many miracles and graces, grant our volunteers the grace to live a glorious mission and return home strong in faith and filled with fervent charity. We beseech you through his prayer

R. Amen

St. Charbel, intercede for us.

Say 1: Our Father... Say 1: Hail Mary... Say 1: Glory Be...

* * *

- Day 5: Prayer :

In the name of the Father, and of the Son, and of the Holy Spirit.

R. Amen.

God, who is infinitely holy and is exalted in your saints, who gave the hermit monk St. Charbel the courage to withdraw from the world in order to live fully in his hermitage the monastic virtues of poverty, obedience, and chastity, we implore you to give us the grace to love and serve you as he did.

(Say your intentions here...)

Lord Almighty, who has shown the power of St. Charbel's intercession by many miracles and graces, grant our volunteers the grace to live a glorious mission and return home strong in faith and filled with fervent charity. We beseech you through his prayer

R. Amen

St. Charbel, intercede for us.

Say 1: Our Father... Say 1: Hail Mary... Say 1: Glory Be...

* * *

- Day 6: Prayer:

In the name of the Father, and of the Son, and of the Holy Spirit.

R. Amen.

God, who is infinitely holy and is exalted in your saints, who gave the hermit monk St. Charbel the courage to withdraw from the world in order to live fully in his hermitage the monastic virtues of poverty, obedience, and chastity, we implore you to give us the grace to love and serve you as he did.

(Say your intentions here...)

Lord Almighty, who has shown the power of St. Charbel's intercession by many miracles and graces, grant our volunteers the grace to live a glorious mission and return home strong in faith and filled with fervent charity. We beseech you through his prayer

R. Amen

St. Charbel, intercede for us.

Say 1: Our Father... Say 1: Hail Mary... Say 1: Glory Be...

* * *

\- Day 7: Prayer:

In the name of the Father, and of the Son, and of the Holy Spirit.

R. Amen.

God, who is infinitely holy and is exalted in your saints, who gave the hermit monk St. Charbel the courage to withdraw from the world in order to live fully in his hermitage the monastic virtues of poverty, obedience, and chastity, we implore you to give us the grace to love and serve you as he did.

(Say your intentions here...)

Lord Almighty, who has shown the power of St. Charbel's intercession by many miracles and graces, grant our volunteers the grace to live a glorious mission and return home strong in faith and filled with fervent charity. We beseech you through his prayer

R. Amen

St. Charbel, intercede for us.

Say 1: Our Father... Say 1: Hail Mary... Say 1: Glory Be...

* * *

- Day 8: Prayer :

In the name of the Father, and of the Son, and of the Holy Spirit.

R. Amen.

God, who is infinitely holy and is exalted in your saints, who gave the hermit monk St. Charbel the courage to withdraw from the world in order to live fully in his hermitage the monastic virtues of poverty, obedience, and chastity, we implore you to give us the grace to love and serve you as he did.

(Say your intentions here...)

Lord Almighty, who has shown the power of St. Charbel's intercession by many miracles and graces, grant our volunteers the grace to live a glorious mission and return home strong in faith and filled with fervent charity. We beseech you through his prayer

R. Amen

St. Charbel, intercede for us.

Say 1: Our Father... Say 1: Hail Mary... Say 1: Glory Be...

* * *

- Day 9: Prayer :

In the name of the Father, and of the Son, and of the Holy Spirit.

R. Amen.

God, who is infinitely holy and is exalted in your saints, who gave the hermit monk St. Charbel the courage to withdraw from the world in order to live fully in his hermitage the monastic virtues of poverty, obedience, and chastity, we implore you to give us the grace to love and serve you as he did.

31

(Say your intentions here...)

Lord Almighty, who has shown the power of St. Charbel's intercession by many miracles and graces, grant our volunteers the grace to live a glorious mission and return home strong in faith and filled with fervent charity. We beseech you through his prayer

R. Amen

St. Charbel, intercede for us.

Say 1: Our Father... Say 1: Hail Mary... Say 1: Glory Be...

* * *

- The Novena has come to an end.

As we near the conclusion of our nine-day devotional and prayer trip to Saint Charbel Makhlouf, it is time for reflection, appreciation, and surrender. We have sought Saint Charbel's intercession during these days, delving into his life, virtues, and spiritual legacy. We have emptied out our souls in prayer, giving our intents and wishes to him, and we have put our faith in his mighty intervention.

Now that we have completed the novena, it is necessary to reflect on the value of this time of prayer and devotion. The novena has allowed us to strengthen our friendship with Saint Charbel and to ask for his intercession in our lives. It has been a time of letting God's grace to enter our hearts and for Saint Charbel's example to inspire and lead us.

Let us explore how Saint Charbel's intercession has impacted our lives during this time of meditation. Perhaps we have seen his miraculous interventions, received his direction, or felt his presence in times of sorrow or despair. Whatever the result, let us show our appreciation for his intercession, acknowledging the many benefits and graces that have poured into our lives.

Individuals' testimony of the power of Saint Charbel's intercession serve as a reminder of his continued presence and active engagement in the lives of his followers. These anecdotes remind us of the miracles and healings that have happened as a result of his intercession, reinforcing our confidence and trust in his spiritual help.

As we end this novena, let us examine how we might carry on Saint Charbel's legacy. His life and teachings call us to increase our love to him and raise awareness of his sanctity. Let us aspire to emulate his characteristics of faith, humility, love, forgiveness, thankfulness, and persistence. May his life serve as a beacon of hope for us, motivating us to live with more passion and commitment to our religion.

Let us send our sincere prayers of thanks to Saint Charbel in these closing hours for his intercession and the ways in which he has affected our lives. Let us thank him for his direction, healing, and spiritual aid. With grateful hearts, we offer up our prayers, intentions, and wishes to God, trusting in His infinite wisdom and providence.

May the intercession of Saint Charbel continue to be a source of consolation, strength, and inspiration in our lives. May his faith and purity serve as a model for us in our own spiritual journeys. As we end this novena, may the benefits and lessons received remain with us and produce fruit in our life.

Amen.

II

Part Two

Biography and Spiritual Legacy of Saint Charbel Makhlouf

Chapter 4

Introduction to Saint Charbel Makhlouf

- Historical Background

To fully comprehend Saint Charbel Makhlouf's life and importance, it is necessary to first understand the historical setting in which he lived. This chapter serves as an introduction, offering a glance into Saint Charbel's sociocultural, ecclesiastical, and political context. We may better grasp the obstacles, influences, and situations that influenced his life and spiritual path if we understand the historical backdrop.

Lebanon in the nineteenth century:

Lebanon in the nineteenth century was a territory distinguished by its cultural richness, social institutions, and religious landscape. It was a period of significant development and transition. Investigate Lebanon's historical context throughout this time period, taking into account its geographical position, the effect of surrounding nations, and the impact of global events on the area. Discuss the many communities that coexisted in Lebanon, such as Maronite Christians, Muslims, and others.

Maronite Christianity:

Within the greater Christian landscape, the Maronite Church, to which Saint Charbel belonged, has a rich history and unique customs. Give an outline of Maronite Christianity, its roots, and growth as a distinct branch of the Catholic Church. Discuss the Maronite Church's spiritual and liturgical activities, emphasizing its strong ties to the Syriac and Aramaic traditions. Explain the importance of the Maronite Church in Lebanon and its relevance in moulding Saint Charbel's spiritual life.

Monasticism in the Maronite Tradition:

Monasticism is important in the Maronite Christian tradition. Investigate the history and relevance of monasticism within the Maronite Church. Discuss the ideas and principles that govern Maronite monastic life, such as prayer, isolation, discipline, and contemplation. Explain the importance of monasticism in the spiritual development of people, especially Saint Charbel's vocation to the monastic life and subsequent journey in the monastery of Saint Maron.

Historical obstacles and Influences:

In the nineteenth century, Lebanon experienced several internal and foreign obstacles that had a tremendous influence on its sociopolitical and religious environment. Investigate the historical backdrop of Lebanon during Saint Charbel's time, taking into account the region's political upheaval, economic challenges, and foreign influences. Discuss how these obstacles influenced people's everyday life, particularly their religious rituals and spiritual interests. Consider how these historical variables impacted Saint Charbel's spiritual journey and the decisions he made.

- Saint Charbel Makhlouf: An Overview

Saint Charbel Makhlouf's life exemplifies faith, dedication, and exceptional holiness. He was born on May 8, 1828, in the town of Bekaa Kafra, Lebanon, to a poor and pious Maronite Christian family. Charbel demonstrated a great sense of spirituality and a strong desire to devote his life to God from a young age.

Charbel took the hard choice to leave his family and worldly interests behind after feeling a powerful pull to the monastic life. He joined the Monastery of Saint Maron in Annaya in 1851, when he began a path of deep spiritual development and change.

Charbel engaged himself in a life of meditation, quiet, and penance inside the walls of the monastery. He accepted the monastic rules wholeheartedly, aiming to adapt his will fully to God's plan. Charbel sought unity with the Divine via intensive contemplation and a life of self-denial, giving himself fully to God's direction and providence.

Throughout his life, Saint Charbel's excellent qualities shined brilliantly. His unshakeable confidence in God's plan and providence demonstrated his great faith. His every deed and contact was defined by humility, as he considered himself as nothing more than a humble servant of God. His life was built on obedience, as he surrendered himself totally to the will of his superiors and the teachings of the Church.

Charbel's devotion to prayer was exceptional. He spent hours in close connection with God, allowing the Divine's presence to pervade his whole body. He received strength, wisdom, and inspiration for his spiritual path from his intense prayer practice.

Saint Charbel is connected with several miracles and heavenly interventions, both during his earthly life and after his death. Through his intercession, thousands of people have received healing, conversions, and answered prayers. Saint Charbel's miracles continue to astound and strengthen individuals who turn to him in times of need.

On October 9, 1977, Pope Paul VI canonized Saint Charbel Makhlouf, recognizing his virtue and the immense devotion he inspired. His canonization attracted international attention to his amazing life and the influence he had on the lives of countless others.

Today, devotion to Saint Charbel is growing all across the globe. People from many walks of life come to him for intercession, attracted to his example of faith, humility, and closeness to God. His life and qualities serve as an inspiration and source of hope to those who come into contact with him.

Chapter 5

Call to Monastic Life

- Discernment and Entrance into Monasticism

T he call to the monastic life is frequently a highly personal and spiritual journey, and it was no different for Saint Charbel Makhlouf. This chapter delves into the pivotal events and choices that led him to choose the monastic life.

Soul Stirrings:

There were stirrings deep inside Saint Charbel's heart that caused him to doubt the road he was on. He yearned for a closer relationship with God and a more meaningful existence. These inner stirrings, which often occur as a consequence of grace, awoke in him a hunger for spiritual satisfaction beyond worldly concerns.

Discernment:

Saint Charbel used the discernment process to further comprehend and confirm his vocation to the monastic life. He went to prayer for guidance and insight from God in order to understand His will. Saint Charbel was able to identify the validity of his vocation by meditation, seeking spiritual guidance, and giving himself to the promptings of the Holy Spirit.

Encounter with the Monastic Tradition:

Saint Charbel was guided to the monastic tradition by divine providence, whether via interactions with monks, spiritual reading, or other ways. These experiences showed him the beauty and depth of the monastic life, and he was inspired by the examples of holy men who had gone before him.

Acceptance of the Monastic Life: Acceptance of the monastic life was not taken lightly. Saint Charbel understood the value of leaving his family, home, and worldly pleasures behind. However, the desire to offer God his whole being and seek a life of greater unity with Him surpassed any ties to the world. Saint Charbel took the choice to follow the call he had sensed with great calm and certainty.

Admission to the Monastery of Saint Maron:

After making his choice, Saint Charbel applied for admission to the Monastery of Saint Maron in Annaya. The procedure of joining the monastery included introducing oneself to the monastic community and asking membership. Recognizing his sincerity and vocation, the community accepted him into their ranks, marking the start of his official journey in monastic life.

Adjustments, Disciplines, and Routines:

Saint Charbel's early days in monastic life were defined by adjustments, disciplines, and routines. With humility and obedience, he accepted the monastic way of life, learning from the elder monks who taught him along the way. These formative years laid the groundwork for his spiritual development and the formation of his distinct charism.

- Life in the Monastery: Asceticism and Devotion

Saint Charbel Makhlouf's monastic life was marked by a deep dedication to discipline and devotion. This chapter delves into the specifics of his daily routine, spiritual practices, and monastic rigors.

Accepting the Monastic Rule:

As a monk in the Monastery of Saint Maron, Saint Charbel accepted the monastic rule as a framework for his life of prayer, labor, and spiritual development. Investigate the precise components of the rule that impacted his daily routine and relationships within the monastic community.

Liturgical Life:

The liturgical life was fundamental to Saint Charbel's everyday life. Describe the monastic prayers, Divine Office, and Eucharistic celebrations that occurred throughout his day. Emphasize the significance of group worship and its role in sustaining his spiritual life.

Prayer and Contemplation:

Saint Charbel's devotion to prayer was outstanding. Discuss the many types of prayer he practiced, such as the Jesus Prayer, quiet contemplation, and meditation techniques. Investigate the importance of isolation and quiet in his desire for a closer relationship with God.

Fasting and Mortification: Asceticism was an important part of Saint Charbel's life as a monk. Describe his fasting habits, abstention from particular foods, and self-imposed mortifications. Explain the spiritual importance of these acts and how they have transformed his path to holiness.

physical Labor and Humility:

In the monastic spirit, Saint Charbel participated in physical labor as a kind of self-discipline and a practical contribution to the community's needs. Discuss the sorts of jobs he did, such as farming, gardening, or other responsibilities within the monastery. Highlight the virtue of humility that he developed via his willingness to do menial jobs.

Despite the focus on contemplative and ascetic activities, Saint Charbel acknowledged the value of intellectual training. Investigate his quest for knowledge, whether through theological studies, spiritual reading, or intellectual debates with other monks.

Monastic Community Interactions:

Describe Saint Charbel's interactions with the monastic community. Discuss the fraternal ties he made, the mutual support and encouragement he got from his superiors, and the spiritual advice he received from them. Highlight the monastery's environment of love, humility, and accountability.

We see Saint Charbel's constant adherence to the monastic disciplines of austerity, prayer, and humility throughout his life at the monastery. His dedication to a life of self-denial and sincere devotion helped him to get closer to God, altering his own soul and becoming a holiness lighthouse for others. We get insight into the path of spiritual development and oneness with God that he exhibited by studying his monastic experience.

Chapter 6

Charbel's Teachings and Virtues

- Key Teachings and Spiritual Insights

I n this chapter, we dig into Saint Charbel Makhlouf's deep teachings and spiritual insights. His holy life and relationship with God produced priceless insights and qualities that continue to inspire and encourage Christians to this day.

1. Emphasis on Personal Prayer:

Personal prayer was highly valued by Saint Charbel as a method of improving one's connection with God. Investigate his teachings on the significance of frequent and ardent prayer, stressing the value of having a personal conversation with the Divine.

2. The Primacy of Love:

At the heart of Saint Charbel's teachings was love. Discuss his focus on the mandate to love God first and one's neighbor as oneself. Expound on his ideas on selflessness, compassion, and the transforming power of love in mending and repairing relationships.

3. The Beauty of Humility:

Saint Charbel exemplified and preached the virtue of humility. Investigate his teachings on accepting humility as a way of spiritual progress and emulating Christ. Emphasize the significance of accepting one's own limits, adopting an attitude of obedience, and living a life of service to others.

4. Embracing the Cross:

Saint Charbel's life was characterised by a profound grasp of the Cross's redeeming power. Discuss his teachings on accepting suffering, bearing one's cross, and linking one's own troubles with Christ's suffering. Investigate his thoughts on finding meaning and purpose in the face of adversity and giving them as a sacrifice for the redemption of souls.

5. Purity of Heart and Mind:

Saint Charbel highlighted the need of purity of heart and mind in order to truly meet God. Investigate his teachings on the significance of practicing virtue, protecting one's ideas, and pursuing inner self development. Discuss his perspectives on the spiritual war against temptation and the pursuit of holiness in all realms of life.

6. Faith in Divine Providence:

Saint Charbel's teachings centered on faith in God's providence. Investigate his teachings on yielding to God's will, trusting in His plan, and depending on His direction and provision. Discuss his insights on the virtue of leaving everything to God's loving care and the tranquility that comes from doing so.

7. Universal Call to Holiness:

Saint Charbel thought that everyone was called to holiness. Discuss his teachings on the possibility of holiness in all vocations and stages of life. Explore his thoughts regarding grace's transforming power and the encouragement to all to strive for holiness in their everyday lives.

- Virtues Exemplified by Saint Charbel Makhlouf

Let us look at the qualities that Saint Charbel Makhlouf demonstrated during his life. His deep spirituality and constant dedication to holiness are proof of the transformational power of virtuous life.

1. Deep Faith and confidence in God:

Saint Charbel's life was marked by profound faith and confidence in God. Discuss how he depended on God's direction, providence, and promises in many aspects of his life. Investigate his steadfast faith in the invisible and his capacity to submit his will to the divine.

2. Humility:

Saint Charbel was famed for his humility, believing himself to be the least of the brothers. Investigate how he demonstrated humility in his dealings with others, acceptance of menial chores, and acknowledgment of his own unworthiness before God. Discuss how his humility enabled him to be receptive to

God's grace and selflessly serve others.

3. Obedience:

Saint Charbel's life was infused with the virtue of obedience. Examine his swift and happy obedience to his superiors, commitment to the monastic rule, and readiness to submit to God's will in all situations. Show how his obedience fostered humility, faith, and a feeling of oneness with the divine design.

4. Prayerfulness:

Saint Charbel lived a profoundly prayerful life. Discuss his unshakable devotion to seeking oneness with God via contemplation, as well as his dependence on prayer as a source of spiritual strength and direction.

5. Purity and Chastity:

Saint Charbel practiced purity, working hard to keep his heart, mind, and body free of sin and worldly attachments. Discuss his chastity commitment, rejection of impure ideas and acts, and awareness of purity as a method of coming closer to God.

6. Love and Compassion:

Saint Charbel was an example of love and compassion for others. Discuss his devoted care for the sick, readiness to listen to and console those in need, and capacity to provide mercy and forgiveness. Highlight how his affection sprang from his great love for God and his understanding of every person's intrinsic value.

7. Endurance and persistence:

In the midst of obstacles and challenges, Saint Charbel's life was defined by endurance and persistence. Discuss how he faced bodily and spiritual hardship with patience and faith in God. Examine his capacity to stay focused on his vocation and his persistent dedication to his monastic life.

Chapter 7

Miracles and Supernatural Phenomena

- Miracles Attributed to Saint Charbel Makhlouf

T hroughout history, Saint Charbel Makhlouf has been associated with numerous miraculous events and supernatural phenomena, showcasing the extraordinary power of his intercession. In this chapter, we delve into some of the remarkable miracles attributed to Saint Charbel, which continue to inspire and strengthen the faith of believers.

1. Healing Miracles:

The intercession of Saint Charbel has been linked to countless healing miracles, where individuals afflicted with physical ailments and illnesses have experienced remarkable recoveries. Share stories of those who were diagnosed with incurable diseases, paralyzed limbs, or debilitating conditions, and witnessed a miraculous healing after seeking Saint Charbel's intercession. Describe the medical documentation, testimonies, and scientific investigations that support these miraculous healings, underscoring the extraordinary power of God working through Saint

Charbel.

2. Intercessions for Spiritual Needs:

Saint Charbel's intercession has also been sought for spiritual needs, leading to profound conversions and spiritual transformations. Share accounts of individuals who, through the prayers of Saint Charbel, experienced a deepening of faith, liberation from spiritual afflictions, and reconciliation with God. Illustrate the stories of those who were trapped in sin or distant from the Church, but through Saint Charbel's intercession, encountered divine grace and were drawn back to a life of faith and holiness.

3. Protection and Guidance:

Many individuals have attributed their protection and guidance in times of danger, distress, or confusion to the intercession of Saint Charbel. Share stories of those who found themselves in life-threatening situations, experienced supernatural interventions, or received inner guidance that they believe came directly from Saint Charbel. These accounts highlight the spiritual presence and powerful intercession of Saint Charbel, bringing comfort, courage, and divine assistance to those in need.

4. Signs and Wonders:

Alongside the healing miracles and intercessions, there have been reports of signs and wonders associated with Saint Charbel. These can include the incorruptibility of his relics, the fragrance of roses or other celestial scents emanating from his tomb, and other inexplicable phenomena. Explore these extraordinary occurrences, emphasizing their impact on the faithful and the deep sense of awe and reverence they inspire.

It is important to note that the Church carefully investigates and verifies these miraculous events before officially recognizing them. The documented cases of miraculous healings, conversions, and supernatural phenomena associated with Saint Charbel serve as a testament to his sanctity and the powerful intercession he continues to offer to those who turn to him in faith.

The miraculous interventions attributed to Saint Charbel Makhlouf stand as a profound testament to his closeness to God and the extraordinary grace that flows through his intercession. These stories of healing, spiritual transformation, protection, and supernatural signs inspire believers to seek his intercession with trust and confidence, knowing that Saint Charbel continues to be a powerful advocate in their lives.

- Supernatural Gifts and Manifestations

There have been tales of supernatural talents and manifestations related with Saint Charbel Makhlouf's life and intercession, in addition to the verified miracles credited to him. These exceptional events provide as more proof of his intimate relationship with God and unique favors. Let us look at some of the most amazing spiritual talents and manifestations.

1. Discernment:
 Saint Charbel was said to have the gift of discernment, which is the spiritual capacity to recognize the activities of the Holy Spirit and discriminate between good and evil. Share tales of

his remarkable insight into the hearts and souls of those who sought his advice, as he provided insightful counsel, disclosed hidden truths, and guided them on their spiritual path. Discuss how his insight has impacted people's lives, offering clarity, healing, and a greater feeling of God's presence.

2. Bilocation:

There have been accounts of Saint Charbel being able to bilocate, appearing in two separate places at the same time. Examine testimonies from people who claim to have seen Saint Charbel appear in two locations at the same time, bringing consolation, advice, or performing acts of healing and kindness. Discuss the significant influence of these bilocation events on individuals who observed them, as well as the faith it instilled in believers' hearts.

3. Ecstasies and Mystical unity:

Saint Charbel's strong spiritual life was often characterized by ecstasies and mystical experiences in which he experienced deep unity with God. Describe these instances in which Saint Charbel was engrossed in prayer and thought, appearing disconnected from the physical world. Discuss the discoveries and insights he gained during these mystical experiences, as well as how they shaped his teachings and conduct.

4. Heavenly scent and shining Light:

Many people have claimed encountering a heavenly scent or the presence of a shining light when visiting Saint Charbel or his grave. Share accounts of persons who have been engulfed with a lovely, heavenly aroma or seen a bright light, which they feel are manifestations of Saint Charbel's spiritual presence. Discuss the significance of these sensory experiences, which evoked a profound feeling of wonder and veneration in individuals who encountered them.

Saint Charbel's supernatural abilities and manifestations demonstrate the tremendous blessings bestowed upon him by God. They provide witness to his holiness and the intimate spiritual relationship he had with the Divine. Saint Charbel's miraculous talents continue to inspire and deepen Christians' faith, reminding them of the limitless power of God's love and the great possibilities that exist inside a life of holiness.

It is essential to view these supernatural gifts and manifestations with caution, remembering that they are not the focal point of Saint Charbel's holiness, but rather expressions of God's grace at work through him. Saint Charbel's life is defined by his unshakeable faith, humility, and dedication to God, all of which continue to inspire and lead Christians to this day.

Chapter 8

Canonization and Recognition

- Process of Canonization

The canonization of a saint is a key event in the life of the Church, acknowledging an individual's holiness and exceptional qualities. In the instance of Saint Charbel Makhlouf, the canonization process was a witness to his life's deep effect and the universal love he inspired. This chapter delves into the process of Saint Charbel's canonization and the Church's recognition of him.

1. Sanctity examination:

The process of canonization starts with an examination of the individual's life, virtues, and reputation for holiness. This study in the case of Saint Charbel included a detailed assessment of his life, including his spiritual journey, teachings, and outstanding qualities. Witnesses were questioned and their testimony were gathered, including those who knew him directly or had information of his life. Church authorities, theologians, and canon law specialists meticulously examined the evidence and documentation pertaining to Saint Charbel's holiness.

2. Beatification:

The beatification is an important stage in the canonization process since it declares the person "**Blessed**" and confirms their existence in heaven. It denotes that the candidate had a heroic life and has been credited with a miracle, usually via their intercession. In the instance of Saint Charbel, Pope Paul VI beatified him on December 5, **1965**. The beatification event drew the attention of the entire Church to Saint Charbel and increased devotion to him.

3. Canonization Process:

Following beatification, the canonization process proceeds with a study of another miracle ascribed to the candidate's intercession. To establish its legitimacy and relation to the candidate's intercession, this miracle must be thoroughly studied, recorded, and authenticated by medical specialists and theologians. Once accepted, the miracle acts as the definitive confirmation of the candidate's sainthood. A miracle ascribed to Saint Charbel's intercession was extensively investigated and finally accepted.

4. Sainthood Proclamation:

The proclamation of sainthood is the climax of the canonization process. It is the Pope's formal proclamation that the candidate is to be honored and worshipped as a saint by the faithful. In the instance of Saint Charbel, Pope Paul VI proclaimed him a saint on October 9, 1977. Saint Charbel's exemplary qualities, holiness, and the genuineness of his intercessory ability were all confirmed in this proclamation. It saw him as a holiness model and a source of encouragement for the devout.

Saint Charbel Makhlouf's canonization not only confirmed his holiness, but also granted formal acknowledgement of his spiritual legacy and effect on the lives of Christians. It affirmed the faithful's dedication and adoration for him and fostered a greater appreciation for his life and teachings. The canonization of Saint Charbel invites the Church and the world to imitate his virtues, seek his intercession, and come closer to God by his example.

- Beatification and Canonization Ceremonies

The beatification and canonization rituals are major events in a saint's life because they signify the Church's formal acknowledgment of their holiness and confirm their intercessory power. In the case of Saint Charbel Makhlouf, these rites were momentous occasions that drew the world's attention to his holiness and secured his position among the saints. This chapter delves into Saint Charbel's beatification and canonization rituals, examining their importance and influence on the faithful.

Beatification Ceremony:

Pope Paul VI presided over the beatification ceremony of Saint Charbel, which took place on December 5, 1965, in Rome. A large number of faithful attended the event, including delegates from Lebanon and Saint Charbel followers from throughout the globe. It started with a somber procession, then prayers, liturgical readings, and the announcement of the papal decision of beatification. The public exhibition of Saint Charbel's face or image, together with relics or personal things, acted as a visual reminder of his holiness. The beatification of Saint Charbel offered the faithful great delight and inspiration as they saw the formal acknowledgement of his heroic virtues and unique position in the communion of saints.

Canonization Ceremony:

Pope Paul VI presided over Saint Charbel's canonization ceremony, which took place on October 9, 1977, in Rome. The ritual drew a large crowd of believers, including pilgrims from Lebanon and followers from all around the globe. The canonization event started with a somber procession of cardinals, bishops, and other dignitaries reciting holy songs. The Holy Father gave a sermon in which he emphasized Saint Charbel's outstanding life, virtues, and miracles ascribed to his intercession. The decree of canonization that followed confirmed Saint Charbel's status as a saint to be worshipped and invoked throughout the Church. Saint Charbel's canonization generated immense delight and a renewed feeling of devotion among the devout, who recognized him as a strong intercessor and an incentive to live a good life.

Influence on Devotion and the Faithful:

Saint Charbel's beatification and canonization celebrations had a significant influence on the devotion and spiritual life of the faithful. The Church's formal acknowledgment of his holiness strengthened the faithful's faith in his intercessory power. Those who previously venerated Saint Charbel as a saint found their devotion strengthened, while others encountered him for the first time and were motivated to seek his intercession. The rituals also highlighted Saint Charbel's exceptional characteristics and his message of faith, humility, and self-sacrifice, urging the faithful to adopt these virtues in their own lives. Pilgrimages, prayers, and the adoration of relics, all linked with Saint Charbel, received increased relevance and appeal.

Saint Charbel's beatification and canonization were watershed milestones that elevated his holiness to the forefront of the Church and the world. They confirmed his intercessory power, encouraged devotion, and served as a permanent reminder of his amazing life and virtues. Saint Charbel continues to captivate the devout, who seek his strong intercession and find inspiration in his noble example.

- Official Recognition of Saint Charbel Makhlouf's Holiness

The canonical acknowledgement of a saint's holiness is an important stage in the canonization process, as it confirms their exemplary virtues, intercessory power, and presence in the communion of saints. In the instance of Saint Charbel Makhlouf, the Church formally acknowledged his holiness through different pronouncements and decrees. We will look at the formal acknowledgement of Saint Charbel's holiness , as well as the importance of these announcements and their influence on the faithful.

1. Decrees of Heroic Virtues:
The Church methodically investigates a candidate for saint-hood's life and virtues, looking for proof of heroic virtue and sanctity. In the instance of Saint Charbel, a decree of heroic

virtues was published, attesting to his exemplary life and heroic virtue practice. This pronouncement recognized Saint Charbel's great sanctity, his dedication to a life of prayer, self-denial, and self-sacrifice, and his unshakeable confidence in God. The heroic virtues proclamation was a significant step in the formal acknowledgement of Saint Charbel's holiness, laying the path for additional investigation and, eventually, canonization.

2. Approval of Miracles:

Miracles ascribed to a candidate for sainthood's intercession play an important part in the process of formal recognition. These proofs of God's favor and the candidate's proximity to Him are symbolized by these miracles. Numerous miracles were recorded and meticulously researched in the case of Saint Charbel by medical specialists and theologians. These miracles were declared real after extensive examination and were regarded as miraculous interventions via Saint Charbel's intercession. The approbation of these miracles confirmed Saint Charbel's holiness and intimate closeness to God.

3. Beatification and Canonization:

The beatification and canonization rituals are the most important formal recognitions in a saint's life. Beatification declares the person "**Blessed**," and canonization calls them a saint. In the instance of Saint Charbel, these were historic events at which the Church publicly acknowledged his holiness and intercessory ability. Saint Charbel's beatification, presided over by Pope Paul VI, and later canonization elevated him to the ranks of the blessed and saints, respectively. These proclamations validated his qualities, intercessory powers, and exemplary life as an example of Christian sanctity.

The Church's formal acknowledgement of Saint Charbel Makhlouf's sanctity laid the groundwork for widespread reverence and devotion. It confirmed the experiences and testimonials of individuals who had observed his intercession and the miracles ascribed to him. The honor also urged the faithful to look to Saint Charbel for inspiration, spiritual advice, and help in their own lives.

The Church formally acknowledged Saint Charbel Makhlouf as a saint through heroic virtue decrees, miracle approval, and solemn beatification and canonization rituals. His holiness continues to inspire people all across the globe, pulling them closer to God and reminding them of the transformational power of a Gospel-centered life.

Chapter 9

The Continuing Impact of Saint Charbel Makhlouf Today

- Shrines and Pilgrimage Sites

S aint Charbel Makhlouf's legacy continues to ring true among the faithful, inspiring devotion and attracting people from all walks of life to seek his intercession and feel his tremendous presence. The creation of shrines and pilgrimage sites devoted to Saint Charbel is one expression of his lasting significance. In this chapter, we will look at some of the most important shrines and pilgrimage locations linked with Saint Charbel Makhlouf, where believers congregate to commemorate his memory, seek spiritual consolation, and pray.

1. Annaya, Lebanon:

Saint Charbel's followers maintain a particular place in their hearts for the hamlet of Annaya in Lebanon. Saint Charbel spent the latter years of his life in the Monastery of Saint Maron, where he dedicated himself to meditation and seclusion. Today, the Monastery of Saint Maron is a popular pilgrimage destination, drawing thousands of tourists each year. Pilgrims come to honor Saint Charbel, reverence his relics, and pray for his intercession. The monastery also has a museum where you can see Saint Charbel's personal things and learn about his life and spirituality.

2. Saint Charbel Monastery, Bekaa Kafra, Lebanon:

Saint Charbel Makhlouf was born in Bekaa Kafra, a highland town in Lebanon. It is the location of the Saint Charbel Monastery, a popular pilgrimage site for individuals looking to strengthen their devotion to Saint Charbel. The monastery is a place of meditation and contemplation, with a respected statue of Saint Charbel and a chapel dedicated to him in the church. Pilgrims flock to Bekaa Kafra to enjoy the serene beauty of the surrounding area and to feel Saint Charbel's spiritual presence.

3. Other Shrines and Devotional Centers:

In addition to the main pilgrimage sites in Annaya and Bekaa Kafra, Saint Charbel's influence has resulted in the development of many shrines and devotional centers devoted to him. These may be found across Lebanon and the globe, especially areas with Lebanese expatriate groups. These shrines serve as focal sites for Saint Charbel devotion and reverence, providing areas for prayer, contemplation, and social worship. They often contain the saint's relics, sculptures, and pictures, enabling worshippers to develop their spiritual relationship with him.

Saint Charbel Makhlouf's shrines and pilgrimage destinations serve as visible reminders of his ongoing presence and the influence he continues to have on the lives of the devout. People may show their devotion, give prayers, and seek consolation and direction in these hallowed sites. They are beacons of hope and inspiration, inviting people to Saint Charbel and reminding them of the transformational power of faith and virtue.

The ongoing pilgrimage to these places illustrates the great popularity of Saint Charbel's intercession as well as the deep effect of his life and miracles. It is a monument to this simple monk from Lebanon's long legacy, who has touched the lives of countless people by his intercessory power and the example of his virtuous life.

- Feast Days and Celebrations

Saint Charbel Makhlouf's feast days and festivals retain a special place in the hearts of his followers. These events allow the faithful to remember his life, ponder on his teachings, and show their thanks for his intercession. This chapter delves into the Saint Charbel feast days and festivals, analyzing their importance and the many methods in which they are honored.

1. Feast of Saint Charbel Makhlouf (July 24):
   Every year on July 24th, the principal feast day of Saint Charbel is observed. It commemorates his death anniversary and provides a particular opportunity for Christians to respect his memory and seek his intercession. Liturgical services at churches dedicated to Saint Charbel are conducted on this day, with prayers, hymns, and readings focused on his life, virtues, and the influence of his spiritual journey. Devotees assemble to celebrate Mass, worship his relics, and pray for their own

purposes and aspirations.

2. Annual Processions:

Many areas, notably Lebanon, arrange annual processions to commemorate Saint Charbel. These processions are often held on his feast day or other major anniversaries in his life. Believers make a somber procession through the streets, bearing pictures or sculptures of Saint Charbel while performing prayers and songs. The procession represents the faithful's faith and devotion, as they publicly demonstrate their love and admiration for the saint.

3. Local Devotions and festivities:

In addition to the official feast day, different local festivities and devotions to Saint Charbel are held throughout the year. Novenas, special Masses, retreats, and other spiritual events organized by churches, religious groups, or devotees themselves are examples. These gatherings allow devotees to expand their grasp of Saint Charbel's teachings, share their personal experiences with his intercession, and build a feeling of community among his followers.

4. International Celebrations:

Saint Charbel's influence has spread far beyond his original area, and his believers may be found all over the globe. As a result, worldwide commemorations and gatherings have sprung up to honor his life and sanctity. These activities may include conferences, retreats, or pilgrimages in which Christians from across the world gather to honor Saint Charbel's legacy, exchange tales of his intercession, and develop a worldwide community of devotion.

Saint Charbel Makhlouf feast days and festivals give a meaningful and practical means for the faithful to interact with his
spiritual presence and seek his intercession. These events serve
as reminders of his holy life, the miracles credited to him,
and the ongoing influence of his intercession in the lives of
Christians. They provide opportunities for prayer, meditation,
and group worship, building a strong feeling of faith and
thankfulness among individuals who seek direction and support
from Saint Charbel.

- Devotion to Saint Charbel Makhlouf Worldwide

Saint Charbel Makhlouf's devotion has transcended geographical bounds, capturing the hearts and minds of Christians
all around the globe. Saint Charbel's intercession and the
inspiration taken from his virtuous life continue to reverberate
with countless people from his home Lebanon to the furthest
reaches of the world. This chapter examines the international
devotion to Saint Charbel Makhlouf, including the many forms
of devotion, the establishment of communities of believers, and
the effect of his spiritual influence.

1. Lebanese Diaspora:

The Lebanese diaspora has played an important role in spread-
ing devotion to Saint Charbel Makhlouf across the globe. As
Lebanese immigrants settled in numerous nations, they brought
their great devotion and veneration for Saint Charbel with
them. They built churches, shrines, and prayer groups in his
honor, forming lively communities of believers who congregate

to revere Saint Charbel, celebrate his feast days, and seek his intercession. These groups act as nexuses for spiritual support and cultural connection among the Lebanese diaspora, reinforcing their devotion to Saint Charbel in their chosen countries.

2. Global Shrines and Devotional Centers:

Saint Charbel's popularity has resulted in the building of shrines and devotional centers dedicated to him across the globe. These sanctuaries serve as places of prayer, meditation, and social worship for Lebanese diaspora groups as well as people from many cultural backgrounds who have established a personal devotion to Saint Charbel. These worldwide shrines often store the saint's relics, show portraits or sculptures of him, and provide chances for pilgrims and tourists to offer prayers and requests.

3. Prayer Groups and organizations:

Saint Charbel devotees all around the globe often create prayer groups and organizations founded on their devotion to the saint. These groups meet on a regular basis to pray the rosary, recite the Saint Charbel novena, and share their personal experiences with his intercession. They develop a feeling of solidarity among believers and enhance their relationship with Saint Charbel by providing a supportive atmosphere for spiritual growth and camaraderie.

4. Online Presence and Digital Devotion:

Saint Charbel's devotion has spread to online platforms in the digital era. Websites, social media websites, and online prayer groups devoted to Saint Charbel enable people from all over the globe to connect, exchange prayers and thoughts, and seek the saint's intercession. For people who are unable to physically visit shrines or engage in local devotional events, these digital places provide as a source of inspiration, encouragement, and fellowship.

Saint Charbel Makhlouf's widespread devotion attests to the deep effect of his life, teachings, and intercession. It crosses cultural and geographical barriers, uniting believers in their love for the saint and faith in his spiritual presence. The devotion to Saint Charbel continues to grow, bringing consolation, hope, and spiritual nutrition to those who turn to him via local communities, worldwide shrines, internet platforms, or prayer groups.

Conclusion

Saint Charbel Makhlouf's Enduring Spiritual Legacy

Saint Charbel Makhlouf's Lasting Spiritual Legacy

Throughout this book, we have looked at Saint Charbel Makhlouf's extraordinary life, spiritual teachings, and intercessory power. Saint Charbel's life is a monument to the transformational power of faith and holiness, from his modest origins in the hamlet of Bekaa Kafra to his profound effect on the lives of countless persons worldwide. In this last chapter, we outline the most important parts of Saint Charbel's life and teachings, emphasizing the lasting spiritual legacy he has left behind.

1. Humility and separation:
Saint Charbel's life was distinguished by humility and a profound feeling of separation from worldly things and goals. He chose a simple life, foregoing worldly luxuries and devoting himself fully to God. His example teaches us the value of trusting God, pursuing spiritual richness rather than worldly prosperity, and establishing a modest and unselfish attitude in our own

70

lives.

2. Prayer and Contemplation:

A cornerstone of Saint Charbel's spiritual legacy is his constant dedication to prayer and contemplation. He spent hours alone with God, conversing with Him and seeking heavenly counsel. His devotion to prayer teaches us the importance of seeking God's presence in the silence of our hearts, as well as the transformational potential of a deep and personal connection with the Divine.

3. Faith in Divine Providence:

Saint Charbel exhibited persistent faith in God's providence, even in the face of adversity. He accepted the hardships that came his way as chances for spiritual development and relationship with Christ. His faith in Divine Providence encourages us to give God our anxieties, fears, and uncertainties, trusting that He will lead and provide for us in all circumstances.

4. Miracles and Healings:

The countless miracles and healings credited to Saint Charbel Makhlouf attest to his tremendous intercession and the great faith of people who seek his assistance. Saint Charbel's intercession continues to offer hope, consolation, and restoration to people who turn to him in faith, from medical healings to spiritual conversions.

5. Global Reach:

Saint Charbel's spiritual impact transcends cultural and religious barriers. His intercessory abilities and teachings have inspired individuals from all walks of life to seek his counsel and aid. Saint Charbel is a uniting figure who reminds us of the universal nature of religion and the power of holiness to bridge divides and bring people together.

As we come to the close of our journey of Saint Charbel Makhlouf's life and teachings, it is clear that his long spiritual legacy continues to touch lives and inspire hearts all across the globe. The reverence of Saint Charbel's relics, pilgrimage to his shrines, and innumerable anecdotes of answered prayers all attest to the significant influence he has had on the lives of Christians.

May Saint Charbel Makhlouf's life and teachings serve as a source of inspiration, direction, and prayer for everyone who seek spiritual development, healing, and closeness to God. May his legacy shine brightly for decades to come, lighting the road of faith.

- Reflections on the Spiritual Significance

Saint Charbel continues to inspire and affect the lives of many people via his firm faith, virtuous example, and effective intercession. Let us ponder some observations on Saint Charbel Makhlouf's spiritual relevance as we end our trip through his history and spiritual teachings.

1. Faith and confidence in God:

Saint Charbel's life exemplifies the strength of faith and confidence in God. His persistent dedication to a life of prayer, asceticism, and total dependence on God's providence inspires us to develop our own faith and submit our lives completely to God's loving care. Saint Charbel shows us that God is loyal in all situations and will lead and maintain us through every hardship and affliction.

2. The vocation to Holiness:

Saint Charbel's holiness quest and focus on characteristics like humility, simplicity, and obedience remind us of our own vocation to holiness. He inspires us to seek for a closer relationship with God and to conduct lives that reflect His compassion and kindness. Saint Charbel's example tells us that holiness is achievable by those who open their hearts to God's mercy.

3. The ability of Intercession:

The many miracles and answered prayers ascribed to Saint Charbel attest to his intercessional ability. He continues to intercede on behalf of individuals who seek his assistance because of his closeness to God. The intercessory power of Saint Charbel reminds us of the significance of prayer and the enormous influence it may have on our lives and the lives of others. He asks us to approach him with confidence, knowing that he is an advocate for our needs before God.

4. Christ's Unity:

Saint Charbel's worldwide reach and the devotion he inspires among Christians from all countries and backgrounds attest to Christ's uniting power. Saint Charbel is a character who crosses borders and unites people in their common faith and devotion. His life exemplifies the universality of the Christian religion and the relationships we have as Christ's brothers and sisters.

5. The Continuity of religion:

Saint Charbel's long legacy serves as a reminder of the historical continuity of religion. Saint Charbel's dedication has endured from his time in the nineteenth century to the current day. It serves as a reminder that the faith we practice today is founded on the foundation created by the saints and faithful who have gone before us. Saint Charbel's life and teachings weave us into this rich tapestry of faith and motivate us to pass it on to future generations.

Let us take the insights on Saint Charbel Makhlouf's spiritual importance in our hearts as we end our investigation of his history, spiritual teachings, and effect. May his example of faith, holiness, and intercession serve as an inspiration to us on our own spiritual path. Following in the footsteps of this great saint, may us seek to live lives of profound faith, confidence in God's providence, and love for one another. Please pray for us, Saint Charbel Makhlouf.

- Encouragement to Embrace Saint Charbel Makhlouf's spirituality

As we near the conclusion of this book, we are asked to accept Saint Charbel Makhlouf's spirituality and adopt it into our own lives. Saint Charbel's life and teachings provide us vital lessons and inspire us to develop in holiness and improve our connection with God. In this last chapter, we invite you to accept Saint Charbel Makhlouf's faith and let it change your life.

1. Embrace a Life of Prayer:

We are urged to emphasize a life of prayer, as Saint Charbel did. Set aside time each day to connect with God, seeking His presence and direction. Allow prayer to be a source of strength, consolation, and inspiration for you on your spiritual path. Incorporate many types of prayer, such as contemplation, intercession, and thankfulness, to enrich your prayer habit.

2. Develop Humility and Simplicity:

Humility and simplicity were important traits in Saint Charbel's life. Accept humility by accepting your reliance on God and your limits. Detach from material goods and worldly distractions that impede your spiritual progress to cultivate simplicity. Accepting humility and simplicity helps us to open our hearts to God's grace and align our will with His.

3. Practice Obedience and Surrender:

Saint Charbel's submission to God's will and obedience to his superiors are strong teachings for us. Learn to pay close attention to God's voice and to surrender your will to His divine purpose. Recognize that obedience to those God has put in power over you is an act of faith and obedience to God Himself.

4. Seek Holiness in Everyday existence:

Saint Charbel's quest of holiness went beyond the monastery and into every part of his existence. Accept the call to holiness in your everyday activities, whether at work, in your relationships, or in your obligations. Strive to live with honesty, compassion, and love, reflecting Christ's light in all you do. Allow your religion to pervade every element of your life, turning everyday occurrences into occasions for grace.

5. Invoke Saint Charbel's Intercession:

As you accept the spirituality of Saint Charbel Makhlouf, call his intercession into your life. Turn to him in prayer, asking for his direction, protection, and help. Entrust your wants, worries, and ambitions to his loving care, knowing that he represents everyone who call on him before God. Allow Saint Charbel to accompany you on your faith journey, knowing that he intercedes for you with tremendous love and compassion.

We expose ourselves to a tremendous experience with God's grace by adopting Saint Charbel Makhlouf's spirituality. May his life and teachings encourage us to pursue holiness, to strengthen our prayer lives, and to live with humility, simplicity, and obedience. May his intercession bring us peace and strength as we face life's ups and downs. Allow Saint Charbel's spirituality to alter us from inside, so that we might be vessels of God's love and carriers of his light in the world.

Saint Charbel Makhlouf, intercede for us and help us on our spiritual path. May we learn from your example and grow in our relationship with God.

Amen.

Made in the USA
Monee, IL
24 July 2024